HOW TO BUILD A **WINNING CAREER GAME PLAN** FOR MID-CAREER WOMEN

Pivot Point

JULIE KRATZ

ISBN-13: 978-1515148241
ISBN-10: 1515148246

Table of Contents

Dedication

I found an old birthday card—one I wrote to my mother when I was in the second grade—titled simply, "Love is you." It was filled with hearts and pictures of things a second-grader would identify as love. When I reflected on this, years later, I thought it was profound. My mother, Nancy, was a survivor. She grew up with humble means. As a single mom, she did not have access to a lot of resources, but she always made sure we had what we needed. Nancy was a great mother. She fostered my own self-awareness and confidence, and always made sure that I had a plan to be successful. Indeed, "Love is *her*."

I remember how we found that card. My mother had a shoebox, organized by year, documenting every detail of my childhood. When she chose to show me the card, she picked quite the setting. I was less than a year into my first "real job" and was introducing her to my new colleagues. She pulled open the shoebox and passed it around to show everyone. I cannot even count how many times I was teased about this—how many times I heard "Love is you." But there is so much more to this concise statement.

Only lately have I begun to realize how true that statement is. In my mind, love was synonymous with her. I was lucky to have a great mother who set an example of a strong woman and, most importantly, a good leader. She helped me to know who I was. She built my confidence and taught me how to succeed in this world. I have often reflected on that statement and only connected it with her. Recently, though, as I have been talking with my colleagues and networking with other women who are mid-career, I have found this statement to have far more application.

"Love is *you*." Knowing ourselves—our strengths and what we are passionate about—is foundational. We have to love ourselves first, before we will ever achieve enduring success. This is the premise of this book. Many women I have interviewed have said that they wrestle with self-awareness, confidence, and having a career game plan to succeed. Typically I dislike generalities about women, but this is true: we often put others' successes before our own, and prioritize others' needs over our own. It is *the disease to please*. To be truly happy, we must begin with ourselves.

I believe that we need to know what "great" looks like in order to be a great leader. Great leaders often build great leaders. I have had the privilege of being around some great leaders in my career, but my mother's leadership influenced me the most. She passed away many years ago. While I was nowhere near ready to face this world without her, she gave me tremendous strength. She inspired me as a single mother who never blamed anyone for our situation. She led with influence—she coached me to discover who I was, where I excelled, and she taught me how to give. I remember being about twelve years old when she sat me down and went over our budget, line item by line item. She said that when we want to go shopping, it goes there, when we go out to dinner, it goes there. I could have input on the decisions we made, but she made the final call. I thought this exercise was normal, but in sharing with friends, I have yet to hear of a parent doing this. What a great lesson in leadership: being transparent, vulnerable, and coaching others in decision-making.

She always advised me that my purpose was to help women. She was proud of my grades through school and my success early in my career, but she told me it was only the beginning. I could do "the business thing," but my real calling was helping women. Until recently, I didn't fully know what she meant. I now know that my purpose is to help leaders through leadership development and coaching.

This book is dedicated to you, Mother. Thank you for helping me to find my true purpose.

Introduction

The Premise

I have attended many women's leadership conferences and, afterward, I usually ask women what they thought about the conference. They most often say that they want more tools to apply what they learned, and they want more time to connect with other women like them. I think that there is a misperception that women just want to sit around and talk, which is very untrue of today's leaders who are women. I have learned that we want a forum to share our everyday stories and lessons with each other, and we want more actionable tools to implement positive change. Leaving one conference, the idea for this book was born 30,000 feet in the air on the back of a napkin.

First, I reflected on the foundation of accomplishments of women. Feminists have been successful at raising awareness and chipping away at the male-dominated business and political worlds. Yet, even as a women's studies minor and a self-assured feminist, I always had trouble with the *doing* part—where we, as women, struggled is connecting the challenges to successful solutions. We are very comfortable stating facts about the gaps—the wage gap, the confidence gap, and the C-suite gap—but we rarely connect these to practical tools to help solve the problem. We will close these gaps when we proactively choose to be part of the solution.

The Purpose

The purpose of this book is to drive change. This is not a soapbox about all the problems facing women; it is not a compilation of stories about successful women far removed from the rest of us. Rather, this book is meant to make an impact by using existing facts to support the rationale, sharing women's stories to help it resonate, and providing actionable tools and strategies to create positive change. In the back of the book, there is a career game plan template that I encourage readers to complete while reading this book. There is no requirement to rush to finish the book and complete the plan. Rather, I encourage women to take time to digest the content, explore strategies that work, and complete the career game plan at their own pace.

I have a theory. Based on the scores of discussions I have had with mid-career, early-career, and late-career women of diverse backgrounds, and in many fields, I have found that we need to hit the pause button and reflect before moving forward.

Countless stats show that the glass ceiling still exists. It's been around since the 1980s and very little has changed. The bottom line is that more women are graduating from college and getting promoted to mid-level managers, but very few make it to the C-suite or to corporate boards. I began my research with this question in mind: How will we move up successfully and transcend that glass ceiling?

The Six Career Game Plan Strategies

Time and time again, mid-career high-potential women told me that they had succeeded in individual-contributor and middle-manager roles because they had the skills necessary to do the job, saw other women advancing at those levels, and had a passion for learning.

As women advance into mid-career, the landscape changes, and there are far less women around. Families become more of a priority, and women may feel selfish pursuing their career advancement. Well-educated, capable performers and proven leaders often leave or check out of the workforce at mid-career, and society accepts it. Please do not misunderstand me; I completely support women taking time to raise their children. The thing is, I have often heard that women chose to leave the workforce because they did not find purpose in what they did, and lacked the confidence and strategy to ask for what they wanted in the workplace. I doubt that men have these struggles to the same extent.

This book is intended to help women take a long look at that daunting glass ceiling. Instead of thinking of ways to break or shatter it, let's use it as a mirror to our advantage. As countless books have been written on breaking the glass ceiling yet it's still there, let's leverage it as a tool instead. Since it is glass, it will be a great metaphorical tool for reflection. The power of reflection has layers—we must first know our authentic selves, find and express our sources of confidence, and build our unique career game plan. Then, sharing that reflection requires us to connect with those who will help us achieve our career game plan, then ask for their help, and continuously improve our reflections by leading with influence. It's like a circle: once we have completed the process and lead with influence, others follow suit and begin the journey of authenticity.

Based on my research, I am recommending six key career game-plan strategies.

The Methodology

The idea for this book was inspired by many conversations with women over the course of decades. I interviewed women in different industries, with an array of functions, and at various stages of their careers for input on this book. I spoke with women in a range of fields—from non-profit leaders to higher education administrators, from millennial achievers to business leaders. Even an FBI agent. I wanted a true representation of today's high-potential woman.

I asked women a series of questions about their motivations, accomplishments, and lessons learned in their early careers (first 10 years), mid-careers (11-20 years), and late careers (20+ years). I also tested the six career game plan strategies with each woman, asking her what each means to her and why it is important.

The input from these fascinating, high-potential women is woven into every page of this book. In reviewing the data from the interviews, a few key findings emerge:

Mid-career is a pivotal point in women's careers. The words women used to describe their early careers tended to be very positive. The top themes were: exciting, exploratory, networking, learning, and tactical. Contrast that with the words used to describe mid-career: challenging, focused, relationships, confidence, and strategic.

Many women described their early careers as full of possibilities. However, 10+ years in, we find ourselves having to learn a new set of skills in order to move to the next level. Often, women are promoted to middle-manager positions because we are high-performing individual contributors. However, the skill set to lead a team is much different from the skills valued in individual contributors. The tactical, get-it-done attitude is no longer as effective, replaced by the need to be more confident, connected, and strategic.

A plan is critical to success. Of the women with whom I spoke, less than 10% had a plan for their careers. While some could articulate long-term goals, or had an idea of what steps were needed to achieve those goals, when I asked if they had a strategy or game plan to manage their career in the longer term, I saw a lot of blank stares. Conversely, when asked if documenting a plan would help accomplish goals, all agreed. We just do not take the time to do it. Those who did have a strategy had experienced recent success, including promotions and new roles aligned with where they wanted to go in the long term— not likely a coincidence. Research shows that when we have a plan, our chances of achieving success is 80% higher.

Collaboration helps us achieve success. I have purposefully chosen to involve equal numbers of women and men in this process of testing the six career game plan strategies. I talk about it all the time, asking others to poke holes, add to it, and make it better. The feedback has been amazing. It has been a collaborative, iterative process. While I had the opportunity to organize and document the journey, I feel truly privileged to have connected with so many people who wanted to help. Involving others in the process is a good thing. We make each other's ideas better. We need to be there for each other. The six career game plan strategies are a continuous process, more like a circle than a linear path. Once we learn to be authentic, express confidence, build a career game plan, connect with purpose, ask for it, and lead with influence, we close the loop and continuously deepen our own authenticity, and spread the word to others.

I believe we have all the data we need to know about the problems women face. Research from sources like Integrating Woman Leaders, Catalyst, and other experts underscores the facts I presented earlier. What I decided to do with this book was package the data, along with the stories from everyday women, to explain how we can, and will, make a difference. When I say "everyday" I do not mean "ordinary;" these are extraordinary women who are all around us—professional women in an array of jobs, at various stages in their careers.

The career game plan strategies are best told through stories and tools. Each chapter covers one career game plan strategy—conveying its rationale and illustrating with stories how it works for everyday women—followed by tools and ideas to make it actionable.

I want this book to drive positive change. My declaration is that through thoughtful self-reflection, and sharing what we learn in the process of that reflection, we will change the game for all women.

The first strategy we will explore is being authentic. The idea is that we must first know ourselves before we can express the confidence needed to build our unique career game plan.

 Be Authentic

Rationale

Authenticity is foundational. To be successful by our own standards, self-reflection and knowing our authentic selves is a critical first step. People are naturally drawn to leaders who are self-aware, ask for feedback, and are connected to a genuine purpose. In my research, I found time and time again that women often do not take the time to reflect and think about what they really want and what they are naturally good at doing. We are much more likely to think of others and how we can help them than to stop and help ourselves. Hearing this repeatedly from successful women made me wonder about how we will get what we want, especially if we do not pause to first think about what we *really* want?

Many women I spoke to said things like, "It's easier to follow the expected career trajectory" or "I find myself being influenced by what other people want from me." When I probed for a deeper purpose, it was often unclear. What did become clear to me was that spending the time to reflect on what we *really* want, what we are *really* good at doing, and our *genuine* purpose is critical.

Without pausing to take an inventory of our natural tendencies and style, strengths, and opportunities, we risk going in a direction that is completely misaligned with where we want to go. I fear that many of us make this mistake. We want to climb the corporate ladder, secure the next big gig, and eventually we stop and look around and we are somewhere we do not want to be. At this point it's natural to wonder, *How did I get here?*

In my interviews with a diverse group of successful women at various stages of their careers, one thing was consistent: very few admitted to regularly reflecting. Yet as I interviewed them, I asked them to reflect on their careers, what had gone well, the successes, and the challenges. I sent them the questions in advance, and many had jotted down notes in preparation of our meetings. Those who had taken the time to reflect beforehand often had much more personal, deeper answers. They had already realized the value of reflection.

The initiative began with me recruiting women, and soon I found that many women were referring me to other women. Some even sent me thank-you notes or bought me coffee to thank me. That was my "Aha" moment. While I thought I had been the one benefiting from their input, these women had also gained value through my coaching. I suspect it is because they discovered more about their authentic selves and yearned for more self-discovery.

Hitting the pause button is okay. Think of it as a "time out" at a pivotal point in a game. Sometimes we just need to take a breath and adjust our game plan.

I love sports. Good sports coaches analyze the stats at halftime and adjust the plan accordingly. The same strategy applies to our careers. Think of our mid-career point as halftime. Many women succeed through mid-career. Perhaps at this point, taking the time to catch our breath, review our personal stats, and tweak our career game plan could help us transcend through that metaphorical glass ceiling. And, it all starts with analyzing the experiences we have had on the career playing field thus far; this analysis is also known as *reflection*.

While reflection requires an upfront investment of time, it saves tremendous time in the long run. The ROI is clear. Through reflection, we're much more likely to connect with our authentic selves, and far more likely to achieve the goals we *really* want to achieve. In addition, knowing one's authentic self naturally leads to improved confidence, which is the real game changer. As with all of the career game plan strategies, being authentic has three simple steps: (1) expand self-awareness, (2) ask for feedback, and (3) know our genuine purpose.

Stories

In the course of my research, women confided in me about their authenticity. These stories highlight the need to expand our self-awareness, ask for feedback, and come to know our genuine purpose.

I spoke with Audra, a mid-career woman, whose career path included jobs in journalism, consulting, and technology. She shared, "Self-awareness has always been hard for me. My managers have always said that I need to work on it. I thought about it, and realized that I was trying to be good at everything because I thought I would have a better chance of success. But what I realized was that I was not focusing on what really gets me excited. What I do now is journal. I write about what I am working on, what I feel, what I struggle with, what I am thankful for, what I am happy about, my friendships, and my boyfriend. It's funny, as I wrote in my journal, I really found myself. What I realized is that my values are not just at work or outside of work. It's a blend."

Both the personal and professional aspects of our lives will benefit from reflection. Through discovering our passions, we discover our authentic selves.

Becca, a high-potential millennial I spoke with reflected, "I am a big believer in trust. I can always tell when someone is faking. From taking the DiSC assessment, I know that I am high on dominance and high conscience. I want things done my way, and have a tendency to be arrogant. I naturally trust myself, but not others. I am not shy about speaking up, and have always been a type A. What I do to maintain my authentic self is try not to think too much. I trust my gut and try not to overanalyze. I am naturally very competitive, which is a strength, but one I need to make sure others come along with my vision."

Through assessments and other tools, our strengths and opportunities to improve are discovered.

A successful healthcare executive, Gwynne, further expanded on the self-awareness and authenticity journey mid-career with her observations: "Be who you are. It is so very important that people see me authentically, and not as hiding significant parts of myself. Do what you say you will do. Be a good listener. Listen not only to concerns that managers and friends have about work, but also get to know them on a deeper, personal level. This takes courage because you will become more vulnerable. The reward will far outweigh the fear. You will have people who are willing to follow your lead when it really counts and the word will spread about your true character without your interference."

Lisa, a high-potential middle manager in consulting, shared her observations: "You have to have rapport and trust with people. I know that I don't ever open up fully unless I feel like I can trust that person and they have my back. It takes time to earn trust. When I make decisions, my boss says, 'I have your back no matter what,' and I know that he will back me up even if he doesn't agree. That has been huge for me. I also use the DiSC, which has been eye opening and helped me better understand where people come from. It helps me with self-awareness. Often, I find that I pause at end of meetings to ask for feedback from people I trust. My perception is not always reality, but it has to be from people I trust. I always frame it with, 'I expect more than just good job, tell me how I did well or could do better.' I have found that when I ask for feedback and I know it is coming, it's easy."

Feedback is an essential tool is being authentic. Through asking for feedback from those we trust, we expand our self-awareness.

As an executive director, Maggie, put it, "Being authentic means saying what you do, and doing what you say. You have to have action behind your words, matched with integrity, and self-awareness. I have found Myers Briggs, StrengthsFinder, and journaling to be useful tools. I learn from my mistakes, and challenge myself to continue to build upon my authentic self. I have built my own personal marketing plan scrapbook with pages dedicated to my Myers Briggs assessment, my passions, and my mission statement."

Tools are available to help us discover our authentic selves. Learning from our mistakes and acting with integrity help us continuously improve authenticity.

Shirley, an experienced career coach shared, "I have always read a lot of books. If you don't know how to do it, figure it out. Over my career, I have found insight in StrengthsFinder and Myers Briggs. Myers Briggs has helped me know my tendencies, and DiSC has helped me know my behaviors. You need to think about tools… in terms of your success, and make a list of items to improve on with pros and cons. At times, I have done my own personal SWOT analysis for my development plan."

Thoughtful analysis of our own unique strengths, weaknesses, opportunities, and threats (SWOT) is a powerful tool for authenticity.

Tools

Here's the fun part, which will make more sense for those who have already done the DiSC assessment. This is not meant to be a checklist of activities to do, but a menu of tools to consider. Remember, this is not a race. It takes time to reflect. Self-awareness is the critical first strategy; please take the time to do this thoroughly. It will set us up for success in the long term.

In my research, I learned that women are hungry for tools in the areas of self-awareness, asking for feedback, and connecting to a genuine purpose.

For each area—self-awareness, feedback, and purpose—there are several tools. For each tool, I will offer a brief description explaining what it is and how it works, with some feedback from women on how they have used the tool. I suggest we review the tools, find a couple good ones, and complete the career game plan workbook in the back of the book. Before advancing to the next chapter, record the answers to the following questions:

- What are my natural tendencies and behaviors?
- What are my natural strengths?
- What are my opportunities to improve?
- What are my passions?
- What is my purpose?

Expand our self-awareness

DiSC®. DiSC assessments are used to help individuals understand their natural tendencies as they relate to four dimensions—dominance, influence, steadiness, and consciousness. The framework is based on contrasting factors that influence our behavior—preferred pace, task-orientation vs. relationship-orientation, and many others. It's a comprehensive assessment with a full battery of proven questions. It is helpful in assessing our styles and informs us about how to flex our style when working with others. I often coach using the DiSC® assessment when working with teams on communication and teamwork.

In the course of my research, women commented that the DiSC® was a tool they used to better understand why they do what they do, and to better understand how to work with others on their teams. Essentially, it takes the mystery out of people, and creates a common language that encourages connecting. I often facilitate team or group workshops with a variety of activities to help women better understand our natural tendencies and learn the art of flexing to others' styles.

Myers Briggs®. Many of the women I interviewed shared that they had completed it in their education at some point. It is similar to DiSC® in that it focuses on personality types based on four indicators. Each indicator has two choices, creating a total of 16 unique styles pertaining to introversion/extroversion, information, decisions, and structure. The difference here is that this is often used introspectively, with tools to uncover possible career paths and align interests with personality style.

Women indicated they have used the Myers Briggs® assessment to better understand their personalities and what types of professions would best align with their interests. Because of its popularity, this is a tool that is easy to share with others to explore similarities and differences. It is simple to take and interpret, and helps us understand how we think, learn, and behave generally. I often leverage this tool in my coaching because it is a simple tool and helps gain a base level of self-awareness.

StrengthsFinder®. Gallup has a list of 34 strengths based on our common talents. They range from Achiever®, Competition®, Analytical®, Empathy®, to Woo® and Learner®, with many more. This assessment tool is similar to those mentioned above in that there are no "right" strengths. The tool prioritizes all of the strengths, with descriptions and themes expanding on the strengths. Similar to DiSC® and Myers Briggs®, this tool helps us recognize the strengths in ourselves and establishes strategies for maximizing our talents, with application in everyday life, along with recognition of others' strengths.

While fewer women had exposure to the StrengthsFinder®, I found that those who did embraced it. Many shared their top five strengths verbatim, and admitted to keeping a sign on their desks to share with others. I often lead workshops or work with clients individually, helping leaders internalize their strengths, explore strategies to better leverage those strengths, and to better understand how we work with others.

Ask for feedback

Feedback is a gift. Often, when we hear the word "feedback," we shudder inside and our body's defense mechanisms kick in. Feedback is a gift when we properly manage expectations. It is important when asking for feedback to assume goodwill. The person sharing feedback wants to help us. The only way we improve is to do some self-reflection and ask those we trust what we could do better.

The best feedback: cites specific, tangible details, is done immediately following an event, and leads to development. An easy way to obtain this is to ask, "What feedback do you have for me about X?" immediately following a meeting or experience. The person we are asking has no choice but to say something. Do not make the mistake of waiting days or weeks or, worst case, until a performance review, because the question loses context and lessens the impact. If we are part of a larger team with hectic schedules, make it a norm to schedule time to talk about what went well, and what could have gone better, but make it as close as possible to the event. And, once we have the feedback, follow up with the feedback provider, and share action steps and updates. We are in charge of our own personal development, and feedback is pivotal to that development.

Women repeatedly shared examples with me of times they had given or received feedback. What they noticed was that the more often they did it, the more normal it became and the less emotional the reactions were. Imagine working in an environment where we do not have to question how we are doing or what people think about us. Who wouldn't want to know where she stands and how to do better?

360 Feedback. A more formal approach to feedback is the 360. This tool is usually automated through an online survey instrument that gathers perspectives from peers, managers, and direct reports. Some women mentioned having done these themselves, or in partnership with their human resources departments. The assessment tools vary, and most cover competencies like leadership, communication, teamwork, strategy, or analytical skills, and usually solicit feedback on strengths and weaknesses in each area. The goal is to generate some actionable steps leveraging our strengths and opportunities to improve.

Women shared varying experiences with the 360. Those who had some additional coaching or support following the process tended to believe more in the process. And, those who shared their results with others on their team also had more positive experiences. The key to the 360 is to manage expectations up front with those whom we are asking for feedback, make it tangible through action planning, and also to share the results with those whom we asked for feedback. People want to feel their time is valued, and those who care enough to participate want to be a part of our ongoing development. Therefore, making a communication plan is critical. Often, I help clients with their communication plans and coach them on how to internalize the 360 feedback. Sometimes the data is a lot to take in, and having someone on our side helping us self-discover the key takeaways helps.

Informational interviews. The informational interview serves two purposes: to get feedback on our overall career direction, and to network and learn more about other roles, functions, and industries. An informational interview is usually structured with the interviewer (you) setting an agenda covering a variety of topics. These can include sharing our own development goals, interests, and strengths, with a series of questions to learn more about what the other person does. Asking good questions and demonstrating genuine interest are keys to a successful informational interview. People love to talk about themselves and, if we can genuinely engage them in the discussion, they are much more likely to help us when we are ready for those positions.

Women who do this well have a goal for the informational interview. In my research, I heard from women that they sought out those influencers in the organization, or those whom they wanted to emulate, and found ways to connect in a meaningful way on a regular basis. A good informational interview leads to feedback on our career game plans, ideas for career strategies, and also long-term access with that individual or other advocates. Some women shared with me that they often asked, "If I am interested in X, who else should I be connecting with?" The goal is two-fold, to gain self-awareness and visibility to other roles, and also to network and connect with purpose, which we will talk about more in Chapter 4.

Know our genuine purpose

Journaling. Many shared that taking time to reflect and journal is powerful. Writing about our experiences day to day, capturing what is going well, what could go better, and thinking about what we are truly thankful for is a great tool to cement our purpose. This usually involves both the personal and professional realms. Women often have difficulty separating the two as they intersect in so many ways. I encourage women to write about anything and everything that is swimming in their minds.

Take an inventory of what we are proud of, what we want to improve focus on, and what and whom we are thankful for.

Women often said that first thing in the morning or before bedtime is a good time to journal. It helps frame the day in a positive way because we are setting the tone rather than logging onto email to react to others. At bedtime, it also yields better sleep habits as we let our brains wind down and set positive, proactive thoughts into our subconscious before drifting off for eight hours of rest. I know most mid-career women do not get this much sleep, but lots of research suggests seven to eight hours of sleep improves our productivity significantly. Our health is a very important factor in building self-awareness and expressing confidence. If sufficient sleep is not currently occurring, I suggest it be built into the career game plan. It's easier to be authentic when we are fully rested.

Passions. Pursuing our passions is often a journey. First, I recommend taking an inventory of our passions to identify and prioritize those that we truly love to do. Ask ourselves, Do I enjoy doing my job in my "free time"? Would I voluntarily show up at work if I wasn't getting a paycheck? I imagine most of us shaking our heads "no" to these questions. Indeed, based on my experience, I have found this to be a rare thing. But it doesn't have to be. I remember it all clicked for me when a client called me on a Saturday, and I gladly picked up the phone and helped talk him through a people problem he was facing on his team. I enjoyed it. The fact that I was going to have a real impact on this person and his team was very meaningful to me. *I did not perceive it to be work.* I was working for free. I challenge us to think of moments when we may have experienced something like this. Keep our minds open to lots of possibilities, asking ourselves, "If I could choose any line of work, what would I do?" Even if it's not feasible, chances are something tangential to that exists and will be feasible one day.

If we know our passions, we are far more likely to connect them to our purpose. Women who know their purpose often shared a tip. They recommended asking those we trust and know well to describe our purpose to us. Sometimes others see things in us that we have trouble seeing. This happened to me when I reached out to a trusted advisor for advice and she told me about a job opening on her team for a career coach. I had never considered that line of work, but she saw something in me that I did not see. It just took me a while to discover it. Take time to reflect on similar experiences.

Once we have found our purpose, write it down. Make sure it's just a few bullets or sentences. Concise and to the point. Test it with those we trust and know well, and if they say, "I get it," chances are we did it right. If not, get the feedback, and fine-tune—it's an iterative process. For me, my purpose is to help leaders through leadership development and coaching. It's simple and easy to remember. When I tell other people, they get it.

Coaching. (Shameless plug here for my profession!) Sometimes it is daunting to go through all of the assessments, gather all of the feedback, and find our purpose on our own. I have coaches, and have benefited greatly from the relationships, and have become more self-aware as a result of our interactions.

A career coach is often hired by a company to help develop high-potential talent. Individuals hire coaches one-on-one as well. It's critical to know what criteria are important and seek a coach who meets those needs. It's a very personal decision. Some coaches drive accountability, others act as sounding boards, others help us self-discover what we want. We need to know our needs, and find a coach who fits those specific needs.

The purpose of the career coach is to help the individual find the answers within herself through the art of questioning. Career coaches intentionally ask open-ended questions, often starting with "what" and "how" to prioritize the individual's desired outcomes, and help others self-discover how best to achieve those outcomes. The key is through self-discovery, individuals are far more likely to achieve the results they desire. The coach simply helps the individual develop the plan, holds the individual accountable, and then guides the individual over the course of the engagement. This is different than a mentor. A coach does not provide advice and has rarely been in the same exact position of the individual. The coach's job is to keep the individual focused, listen to the individual and help her self-discover how to solve her own challenges, which is far more sustainable over time. The old adage, "Give a man a fish and you feed him for a day; teach a man to fish and you feed him for a lifetime," sums this up well—for men *and women*.

Before proceeding to Chapter 2, take some time to reflect on these five areas: natural tendencies, strengths, opportunities to improve, passions, and purpose. Through my coaching, I have found purpose to be the most profound question. This will be the essence of our plans, so deep reflection is critical.

The next tool we will explore is expressing confidence. Confidence is the game changer in our career game plan.

Express Confidence

Rationale

Now that we have hit the pause button, and have completed the first strategy of the career game plan, we will leverage our authentic selves through expressing confidence. The reason that this is also so foundational is that if we do not believe in our unique strengths and purpose, it will be difficult for others to buy into to our career game plans. There is an incredible amount of data citing the confidence gap women have compared to men. Studies have concluded that women are far less likely to apply for jobs than men who are equally qualified. We rarely negotiate salaries. We count ourselves out before we even have a chance.

As with all of our career game plan strategies, I do not want to focus on the problem, but rather the solution. The goal of this strategy is to better equip us with ideas from everyday women and tools that help express a higher level of confidence. Confidence is essential to achieving long-term success. Unlike our natural tendencies we discovered in Chapter 1, confidence is an area over which we have control; we can improve it with applied and intentional focus. Our authentic, positive, and proactive self-image will fuel our confidence.

Among the high-potential women I spoke with, many expressed a very high level of confidence. Sometimes I was even a little taken aback by it. I found myself feeling uncomfortable at times asking very successful women for their time. What I noticed in reflecting was an improvement in my own confidence and comfort over time. As the conversations became more routine, and I had success, it fueled my confidence. I believed in myself and the purpose of this book. As women validated the six career game plan strategies, I felt inspired. I felt confident. The thing that I have realized along this journey is that knowing myself, what I am good at, and sometimes what I am not so good at, along with my purpose, helps me build rapport with others. The more aware and confident I am in expressing myself, the more others respond to me. It's okay to state what we are good at doing. And it's okay to admit the things we are not so good at, or do not enjoy as much. And, once we know our purpose, expressing it confidently is key. People respond to confidence. It engages others. It motivates others to help us.

Back to our sports analogy. What is something else that successful coaches have in common? They are extremely confident. It makes sense. Their players have to buy into the game plan for it to succeed. So, as we are reflecting on the first half of our own careers, it's important to come out of the huddle with a smile and our head held high. It signals to others that we know what we want. We will play a great second half. One common trait of women CEOs is most have a sports background, and many were captains of their teams. This is not a coincidence. These women have much higher confidence because of their ability to handle challenges and achieve success through a team. They carry themselves more confidently and people want to follow them.

As with all of the career game plan strategies, there are three simple steps for this one as well. To express confidence, (1) know who and what fuels our confidence, (2) surround ourselves with people and experiences that reinforce our confidence, and (3) proactively seek out people and experiences that challenge our confidence. The idea here is to leverage self-awareness about our own confidence, then reinforce and challenge it through people and experiences.

Confidence does not happen in a vacuum; it evolves over time. We can be on top of our game one minute, and then something or someone can rock it, if we let them. Proactively challenge ourselves to maintain that confidence. Get out of the comfort zone. If we are there, it's not going to last. It's time to embrace the challenge. It fuels our confidence once we break through barriers and succeed. It helps us pivot up to the next level.

Stories

A late-career human resources leader, JoDee, reflected on her mid-career with a smile. "I have learned over time to leverage my strengths. I was able to use my strengths as a Maximizer, along with Positivity and Strategic. I had a vision for our HR department, and was able to see it through. I delegated, recruited, and hired the right people that had a huge impact on the culture. I believe my confidence developed over time by being around good leaders and mentors. I had to be confident when I asked those leaders and mentors for help. I also had to be a little bit vulnerable. What I found in being vulnerable was that when I asked for help, I got more confident. I still remember one of my evaluations where a partner commented that I had a lot of self-confidence. From that day forward, it multiplied."

Confidence is fueled over time, from within and through others. It has a multiplier effect on who we are and how we interact with others.

Kola, a published author heading into mid-career shared, "Curiosity and the long-term potential for success has motivated me throughout my career. Curiosity has motivated me in the sense that when I think of something I want to achieve career-wise, I become very inquisitive about how to make it happen and will usually give it a shot. *Sometimes I win, and sometimes I learn.* The long-term potential for success is also a big motivator for me. I'm okay with taking risks in the short term if I believe that the payoffs would be significant in the long term. I wouldn't climb a ladder that is leaning against the wrong wall just because it feels safe. I'm very proud of becoming an author of a book that has done very well both in the US and abroad. I'm also thankful that I know that communication is one of my strongest assets. I think it would really bother me if I had no clue of what skills make me stand out."

Knowledge of our strengths and leveraging them is pivotal. Taking strategic risks leads to success and learning.

An operations leader, Stephanie, approaching mid-career shared, "Know your facts and understand the facts. I always prepare diligently for meetings or presentations. I ask for assistance if I do not know something that I need to know, and involve others in the process. I ask things like *what do you think* or *help me understand.* You have to be confident enough to ask because you might be missing something. Also, body language is very powerful with expressing confidence. I have heard about the superman pose, where you place your hands on your hips, forming triangles at your sides. I try hard not to cross my arms. People really respond to it."

Many women shared body language examples like this. Studies have shown that those who cross their arms before interviews are far less likely to get the job than those who do the Superman pose before an interview. It helps us feel more confident, and what is more important in a job interview. It certainly is not the time to be humble.

Nikki, a small-business owner and power networker shared with me, "Reach up to mentors, find those that have done what you want to do and connect with them. I seek out those that make me feel a little uncomfortable because they will stretch me and challenge me. I have a network where I can get validation from others when I feel down. Anytime I go through a funk, I sit down and remind myself *why I do what I do*. I have a daily gratitude or reflection on the little things. When I do something new, I often journal what I feel good about and recognize myself. I also have an accountability partner. If you feel down on yourself because of your image or you just need to get weight off, think about how will you do it and get someone to hold you accountable and celebrate with you. You need to have go-to people that you respect to make sure you get it done."

Leverage our purpose to fuel our confidence. Surround ourselves with those who build our confidence, and those who challenge it.

Tools

Before advancing to the next chapter, record the answers to the following questions in the back of the book:

- Who fuels my confidence?
- What fuels my confidence?
- How will I leverage these people or experiences to reinforce my confidence?
- What people or experiences challenge my confidence?
- How will I proactively seek out these people or experiences that challenge my confidence?

There are three simple steps for the expressing confidence chapter. First, (1) we need to know who and what fuels our confidence, then (2) surround ourselves with those people and experiences that reinforce our confidence, and (3) proactively seek out those people and experiences that challenge our confidence.

Know who and what fuels our confidence

Who are the people that help us recognize our strengths and discover our passions and purpose? Knowing this is pivotal. Chances are we all have a strong following of some sort. People we have worked with in the past, family members, childhood friends, and networking contacts are possibilities. They come from everywhere. They often are the people in our lives who make us feel good when we have a bad day, or offer words of encouragement when we need it. These people are vital to our confidence. My mother still fuels my confidence. When I feel my own confidence slip, I remember her stories and her example to drive me forward.

Likewise, we are shaped by our experiences. Think about the experiences throughout our career, which ones fueled our confidence. For me, knowing my DiSC® style and StrengthsFinder® results, being high D and an Achiever®, results really matter for me. For better or worse, results drive me, they fuel my confidence every day. I remember reflecting on this a few years ago. I was growing impatient with my career. I was not advancing as fast as I wanted and really let it take a toll on my confidence. It was a vicious circle. The less results I achieved, the less confidence I had. It was self-perpetuating. I realized through my career coach that I need to diversify my sources of confidence beyond just results. For me, it's now more about being a good mother, earning the respect of my husband and mentors, and inspiring leaders to be better leaders. It is far more than just results. I recommend we tap into our sources of confidence—the people and experiences that shape us—and really dig and explore, and identify at least three to five for each people and experiences.

Surround ourselves with those people and experiences

Let's take our confidence a little further, and add some more fuel to it. Our confidence is almost like a fire, people and experiences are like the kindling that helps it ignite. Adding more of these types of people and experiences leads to a much bigger fire, or level of confidence. Fires burn much better when the kindling is close to the flame, much like we are far more confident when surrounded by our sources of confidence. In this case, that is the people or experiences that help us be the best possible person. Imagine our virtual fires, taking those people and experiences that most effectively fuel our confidence, let's find ways to strategically add them to our fires. This is done in a variety of ways. Brainstorm common interests with those people, plan times to connect with them more regularly, or create a networking group with others that will also drive confidence. I love the idea of accountability partners. Those people who fuel confidence are fantastic accountability partners. An accountability partner is there to share successes, ideas, and challenges.

For experiences, I recommend really digging here for common themes. Perhaps it is being prepared, as one woman shared with me. For me, it was results. Once we know the source, we can capitalize on it like crazy. It needs to be a part of the routine. It needs to be a part of everything we do if that truly drives confidence. For my results driver, I need to have goals to set expectations and metrics to measure the results to be more confident in everything I do. I have a vision board with weekly and monthly goals to do this. I feel so confident when I check something off the list.

Positive affirmations are also an excellent tool to express more confidence. Women I spoke with often mentioned gratitude journals. It can be a great way to start the day, or a visual to display in the office or home. One of my favorite affirmations is to surround myself with positive people. I have it on my office wall to remind me. While writing this book, I also had a positive affirmation, "People love reading my book," above my computer. When I encountered the occasional writer's block, I looked at it, smiled, and typed away.

The impact of being positive is a game changer. It is pivotal to our career game plans. Women I coach often wrestle with positivity. It is much easier to put ourselves down than to build ourselves up. As we transition from authenticity to confidence, we must also transition our mindset to a positive, proactive one. If we find ourselves having negative, confidence-deterring thoughts, we must extinguish them immediately. To do this, I coach leaders to first, recognize the negative thought we are having. Then, quickly push it out of our mind, replacing it as quickly as possible with a positive thought. I have a bank of positive affirmations I use to replace negative thoughts; "I maintain focus" and "I am a sought-out professional" are a few. If negativity persists, as it has for many of my clients, I highly recommend journaling until we can fully discover the source of the negativity. After many years of negative thinking, this takes time to undo. The words we tell ourselves matter. If we tell ourselves that we will think positive, we will. Tell ourselves until we believe it. Do a positivity challenge, tallying positive thoughts in a day. Make it fun. After a while, it becomes routine.

Proactively seek out people and experiences that challenge our confidence

Conversely, naysayers are not likely to be the types of people that fuel our confidence. Speaking of naysayers, those that challenge us can have quite an effect on our confidence. Rather than give our power to them, let's harness it and regain control of it. My career coach often reminds me that *only I have the control of my own confidence.* I remember thinking about this, and realizing how silly it was that I would consciously let someone else derail my hard-earned confidence. But, in speaking with many women, I heard many share this experience: some said it was the bully that often railroaded the team with his or her ideas, others shared it was someone whom they really respected and admired, but felt so inferior to. It can come from anyone or anything. With self-awareness comes the realization of confidence awareness. When it gets shaky, take a timeout, and discover the reason. Maybe it's someone or something that is taking us off track. Reflect further on our opportunities from the being authentic career game plan strategy. Explore where we want to improve. These areas are often confidence barriers.

Once we know who and what challenge our confidence, let's retake control of it. One woman reflected on an experience that rocked her confidence. She said that she recognized it in meetings where there was a male-dominated audience. She felt her confidence wither in this setting. She said that emotional intelligence was a helpful tool, in that she could recognize the confidence shift, and rather than let her emotions hijack her confidence, she took control of it through positive affirmations. She reminded herself mentally of her successes, expertise, and capabilities, and leaned into the team, and carried the discussion forward. She added value to the team in ways that only she could add value. She listened to others, asked good, open-ended questions, and expanded upon what was said. That's confidence.

As with all of our career game plan strategies, there are a few tools sprinkled in here that career women have suggested. One mentioned earlier, the Superman pose, really does fuel confidence. Try it for a day, being conscious of where we place our hands, placing them on our hips with our elbows forming triangles. Do it as much as possible, and take an assessment of our confidence at the end of the day. It's remarkable. As a facilitator of leadership development, I consciously do this at least 20 times in a given day when in front of an audience of managers. It not only boosts my confidence, but it prevents me from distracting the audience with my hands and keeps my posture tall and poised.

One more tool: be vulnerable. This seems a bit counter-intuitive. Just as we did with the naysayers, we can turn a negative into a positive. Being authentic, we better express and share areas where we might not be as strong. This is a good thing. People respond to vulnerable leaders. No one is perfect, and people like to feel needed. Sharing with others, "I am good at X, but not so good at Y" is totally fair. I often share my vulnerabilities with my clients. I am not very good with details. So, I ask for help with this. I smile when I say it, and hold my head high. I acknowledge the weakness, but I do not focus on it for long. What's powerful about this is once people see a willingness to admit vulnerability, they feel safe and empowered to do the same. We build trust, and make others feel important. Those naysayers do not stand a chance against that. We will expand on vulnerability more in leading with influence in Chapter 6.

The next strategy we will explore is building our winning career game plan. With our improved sense of confidence, this will be much easier to do. It will also give us the plan needed to share our reflections and connect with purpose.

Chapter 3

Build a Career Game Plan

Rationale

Likely the most important part of the six career game plan strategies is actually building the plan. The rationale here is fairly obvious, but important to spell out. Very few mid-career women have a plan. We lack goals and strategies to get what we want, or an understanding of what areas we need to work on to get where we want to go. I heard this so many times from women late career—"I looked around and had ended up somewhere I did not want to be"—it still rings in my ears. It really is the premise of this book.

We'll never get to where we want to go if we do not have a plan. I am always so puzzled by this. If this is so obvious, why has it not been implemented? More than 90% of the high-potential mid-career women I interviewed did not have a plan. When I questioned this, I usually received a wide-eyed look, sometimes followed by a sigh. The impression is that this is a lot of work. This seems like a daunting task, which is a complete misperception. A good plan is simple. It's easy to communicate. It's visual and clear. When people we trust and admire look at it, they say, I get it. It custom fits us and where we want to go. It is no more than one page. For those of us tempted to add appendices outlining every detail and rationale for our strategy statement, goals, competencies, and actions, please resist the urge. It only confuses people and makes more work for us. Focus and simplicity are essential.

So, remembering it is halftime of our career, and keeping in mind how important coaching is to success, what do successful sports coaches do to their game plans at halftime? They revise it. After some sort of speech setting the stage of the next half's strategy, good coaches often make bold statements about the outcome of the next half, rallying the team to a common goal, then they usually get out a white board or tablet to share the plan. They share their vision with the team through drawing out the Xs and Os, with arrows illustrating the new plays. Having a clear visual to align the team is key. The coach is able to set the tone proactively for the next half because he or she has a plan.

To build our plans, there are four easy-to-follow steps. First, (1) craft a pivot line statement, then (2) set our goals, followed by (3) prioritize the competencies needed to achieve our goals, and (4) determine the actions needed to reach our goals. Once we set up our pivot line in a concise statement, and the direction we want to go with our goals, the rest is more like a gap analysis to fill in the blanks of what is needed to get there. Knowing our authentic selves will be pivotal here. Our natural tendencies, strengths, opportunities to improve, passions, and purpose are the basis for our goals. They are the drivers of who we aspire to be. Being authentic is a continuous process, one that requires a plan to maintain and grow upon. Our confidence will also play a key role, because we must challenge ourselves to be assertive with our plan.

It is easy to set table stakes for goals. Something like, "I want to be a leader" or "I want to volunteer more" or "I want to spend more time with my family." Those are great wants, but they are not specific, nor are they measurable. Words like "want" and "will" also weaken our goals. They make them sound like they are only achievable in the far distant future. We'll never know when we reach our goals if we do not challenge ourselves and set a clear picture of what the finish line looks like.

Then, we prioritize the competencies—skills, behaviors, or attributes—needed to meet our goals. For those competencies that are highest in priority for improvement and most critical to our successful achievement of our goals, we must fill the gaps and build our tactics and action plans to close them. This is the "doing" part. Finally, creating simple action plans with detailed steps, resources required, and a timeline completes the career game plan.

As we near the mid-point of the six career game plan strategies, we need to also be thinking about how we will share this plan with others. This is the essence of the pivot point. The career game plan document is critical. It has all the detail we need to know what to do. The beauty of it is that it is so simple, that it is also easy to share with mentors, family, coaches, and anyone who will help us get there. It's the tool that will help us ask for what we want, and lead with influence so that others follow us and begin their own pivot point journey.

Stories

A go-getter higher education administrator, Karen, shared, "If you had asked me in law school where I wanted to go, I would have said that I was already doing the job I thought I wanted to do. A good mentor once coached me that a career is a lattice not a ladder. Often, we sell ourselves short and do not think ahead. It creates big problems later when we have a *where do I go from here* moment. It's been difficult for me to build a plan because of the uncertainty of my husband's career. We are a dual career family. Instead of changing careers completely, I thought about possibilities within my current role. Recently, I asked for a new responsibility, knowing that the head of the department might be hesitant. I knew what I wanted to do and expressed confidence and was direct. I prepared by getting a good understanding of the job description. I then explained what I would like to do, how it would benefit the department, and had a good business case. It was easy then to negotiate a salary increase because I had a plan, and I knew the range and asked for what was fair."

When women prepare and have a plan up front, the results are staggering.

Elise, an executive coach extraordinaire stated, "I know how important it is to write down goals. I have tried 16 times to write my business plan, but I am doing well without one. Intentionality is key about what I need to do to be successful. I need to be focused on what is important. Although I did not have a formal plan, I knew credentials were important to my coaching business. I read a great book, *Multipliers*, and emailed the author, asking to become a certified Master Practitioner. She said yes. This was a pivotal moment for me. You have to think about what's important—*what's next*. My one goal has always been to be profitable without having to be on the road more than a few days a week. I intentionally choose to do things that help me achieve that goal, and avoid other activities that do not help me reach that goal."

Goal setting helps us focus our finite time on the things that matter.

An FBI Operational Specialist, Sirena, expanded on this point, "We are all unique. And, I recognize it's tough to do the hard things. At my mid-career point, I looked around and realized I was so unhappy. So, I took some time to reflect, and completely changed careers, moving from a senior leader at a Fortune 500 company to the FBI. While it was hard for me to start over mid-career, I remained humble, and asked myself *what do*

I want? By answering that question, I had a good set of guard-rails on what I wanted, and what I did not want. Money no longer motivated me. Purpose was more important. I have always been passionate about helping children, and my role with the FBI allows me to help with child trafficking and save lives. I am now doing what is aligned with my ethics and values." Our purposes drive our plans. Simply asking *What do I want?* provides much of the detail for our plan.

Sophia, a savvy marketing director in financial services told me about her development planning process, "I have a development plan. I like to have one- and three-year goals. I edit it on an annual basis and check for achievement of the goals. My one-year plan is more firm, and my three-year plan is more aspirational. You can have a five-year plan, but it's more of a pie in the sky. I care more about the action steps needed to reach my goals, and the behaviors needed to achieve the goals. I focus on areas of development and how to get there. This process helped me with my recent promotion. I had not managed people previously, and was a high-potential individual contributor, but management was hesitant to promote me to director because it required managing people. I knew I needed to show my potential, so I asked to manage a summer intern and had a great project for a business case. After successfully managing the intern, management could see I was a good leader. I was promoted soon after, while pregnant. My manager did not drive it, *it was all me.* I had to prove myself first."

In this case, one of the few women who had a plan attributed her success to proactively building a plan with goals, behaviors, and action steps needed to make it real.

Tools

When answering these questions, think in terms of three years from now. One year is often too tactical, and five years is too hard to forecast. For this strategy, since it is the career game plan, there is a one-page document in the back of the book to complete once our plan is ready to share.

- What do I want?
- What are my goals?
- What competencies are needed to achieve my goals?
- What actions are needed to reach my goals?
- What resources will I need to implement the actions?

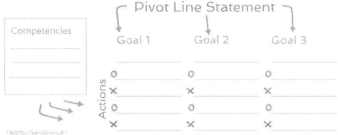

Craft a pivot line statement

For this to be done well, the pivot line statement must be concise (140 characters or less), proactive, positive, and present tense. Think of the pivot line statement as our three-year future goal said in present tense: "I am a successful <fill in the blank>." It answers the question, "What do I want?" At the time of writing this book, my pivot line statement is, "I am an expert in leadership development facilitation and career game plan coaching." It's 71 characters, which is easy for me and others to remember. It goes on my business card, social media, or anywhere relevant to my career game plan. It's my elevator pitch at networking events. People know what I am good at when they hear it. Honestly, because I had a good understanding of my natural tendencies, strengths, opportunities to improve, passions, and purpose, and assessed my sources of confidence, it was really easy to write this down. I suggest sharing our pivot line statements with others, and tweaking based on feedback, as with all of the tools in this book. If people get it, great. If they do not it the first time, edit, and try again.

Set our goals

Goals need to be SMART—specific, measurable, achievable, relevant, and time bound. I recommend keeping it to three or fewer goals. All goals align to the pivot line statement. The process is simple. Just ask ourselves, what would need to be true for the pivot line statement to be realized? In other words, what goals would have to be achieved for that statement to read truthfully? Goal setting is a skill on which I often work with my clients. My business owners and leaders struggle to set true SMART goals. As most are familiar with the framework, we often end up with aspirational statements or immeasurable goals. Testing these goals is pivotal to the plan's success.

For me, knowing my pivot line statement, outlining my vision for the next three years was a simple task. I knew what needed to happen to make my pivot line statement true. In the next three years, I needed to (1) develop and promote three coaching tools for my coaching business, (2) publish two best-selling books on leadership development, and (3) coach 100 high-potential mid-career women on their career game plans. For me to be a leadership development and career game plan coaching expert, I needed for these things to happen in the next three years. I have them all written on my white board in my office to keep them in front of me, along with my pivot line statement. I recommend that once we write our goals, double-check that they are SMART.

- How specific is the goal so that I will know when it has happened?
- How measurable is the goal with at least one number or metric to describe success?
- How achievable is the goal, not to say it is not challenging, but how genuinely attainable is it?
- How relevant is the goal, meaning how will this impact my career game plan when this happens?
- How clear is the goal on when this needs to happen? I recommend three-year goals with annual sub-goals built in if further detail is needed.

If we answer yes to all of the above, it's time to move on to competencies.

Prioritize the competencies needed to achieve our goals

Once we have a just a few critical goals, the gap analysis begins. Competencies are the arrows on our career game plans. They feed into the goals and actions. By asking the question, *To achieve this goal, what competencies are necessary?* we position ourselves to achieve our goals and actions. Again, competencies are behaviors, skills, or attributes. When defined correctly, we can visualize these. In other words, we know what "good" looks like. If communication is a high-priority competency, we would likely cite behaviors like active listening, the ability to ask open-ended questions, and refrain from giving advice or jumping to solutions for them. We would then rate ourselves on the ability to perform on those behaviors, or better yet, leverage the feedback from earlier to assess ourselves.

If we wanted to be scientific, we could do a 2x2 matrix, rating "importance of meeting my goal" on one axis and "my ability to perform" on the other axis. In the spirit of simplicity, I suggest we evaluate both importance and performance. The approach is personal. To keep us realistic, I recommend we target no more than three competencies of focus. More than that, and it's difficult to focus. By prioritizing what is really important, we keep the career game plan achievable and simple to communicate.

When I reflected on the competencies need to achieve my goals and fulfill my pivot line statement, I brainstormed a comprehensive list—written communication, leadership, presence, customer focus, sales, marketing, collaboration, influence, initiative, and follow through. I encourage us to list at least ten to prioritize. Then, I assessed each based on importance. I quickly de-prioritized a few as secondary competencies—sales and marketing—and tasks on which I could collaborate with others. I knew that confidence, written communication, and presence were most impactful to me achieving my goals. Then, I assessed my performance in these areas. Based on importance and performance, I decided to prioritize influence, presence, and confidence. This does not have to be a scientific method. Do what feels right. For me, I am consciously working on my ability to influence others through networking and social media, command executive presence in facilitation through body language and insightful stories and questions, and maintain strong poise and confidence in my coaching business. Those competencies drive the most impact for my goals, and will be improved the most over the three-year time frame for my plan.

Determine the actions needed to reach our goals

Action planning is next. These are the X's and the O's of the career game plan. The blocking and tackling activities. For each goal, keeping in mind the competencies needed and performance against it—what needs to happen for the goal to be met. Keeping with our theme of simplicity, perhaps each goal and competency has an action plan, or some join together. The action plans for the goals are likely to be quite tactical steps for the next one to three years. The competency action plans may be more focused on our personal development. They may be a bit more strategic and cite things like learning, developing new areas of expertise, or networking to help us connect with purpose and share our plans.

For me, a white board is an effective way to document the goals, competencies, and action plans. The white board in my office has each goal written vertically, and I have mapped out action steps for each month this year to progress towards my goal. Later in the year, I will build out the action plans for the next calendar year. It is a bit daunting to predict all the action steps for the next three years. My advice is to document action steps as far into the foreseeable future as we feel comfortable. If we are uncertain, or there are contingencies, map out the first series of activities with a sub-goal to check in, and then revise the action steps once we get there. There is a template in the back of this book that is useful for sharing our reflections.

The final step for a career game plan document is resources. I encourage us to think first about what needs to happen before we think about the constraints. A good question to make sure we are challenging ourselves to think past false assumptions is, "Based on what?" If we have done a good job with a truly SMART goal, this has likely already been considered. Time and money are important. Depending on the level of constraint, prioritizing the budget and time requirements by potential impact is one way to prioritize. As with all of our career game plan strategies, seek input or coaching if this is difficult. Others want to help.

The power of positivity and knowing our purpose is a true demonstration of our reflection. Once we have taken the time to reflect, be authentic, express confidence, and build our winning career game plans, we have the ability to transcend the metaphorical glass ceiling to share our reflections with others. Now that we have a documented plan, it's easy to share it with the right people who will help us. This is also known as connecting with purpose. Before moving onto the next chapter, be sure to complete the career game plan template in the back of the book.

Chapter 4

Connect with Purpose

Rationale

We have our winning career game plan in hand, and we're ready to make it happen. We've reflected, and are ready to share that unique reflection with the world around us. Instead of shattering that glass ceiling, we're going to transcend it. Here's the key to making it happen. Rather than tactically sharing our reflections with anyone and everyone willing to listen, let's be strategic about whom we choose to collaborate with on the plan.

In speaking with successful career women, I heard again and again about the importance of being strategic mid-career. The tried and true "get-it-done" attitude is not as effective once we reach our pivot point mid-career. The women I spoke with also considered relationships a strong key to success. It's less about networking, and more about connecting. So, when we combine strategy with relationships, we get connecting with purpose. Contrast this with collecting contacts. Many admitted to knowing the LinkedIn lions, those who comb the web, and connect with any and all who are willing to connect. So much time is spent pursuing contacts, rather than *connecting with the right people*.

The women I interviewed recommended another, more strategic approach.

It's the halftime of our careers, and we have the winning plan for the second half in our hand. How will we achieve it? When asked this question, the resounding answer women gave me is through people. We need a team around us to help us win the game. The team we enlist provides coaching, mentoring, and advising. Imagine a sports coach on the sideline at a pivotal point in the game. A player comes over to the sideline, talks to the coach, and is heading back into the game. What physical gesture is commonly bestowed upon the player? As women, we always seem to find this puzzling, but at our pivot point, we need a smack on the rear sometimes. In our careers, these often come from a team of people who help us to keep our head in the game.

Since our time is finite, it's important that we spend it with the people who will advise us, mentor us, or coach us. Even though we will be selective with whom we collaborate on our plans, diversity is important. We need a diverse team. Think of these people as our career game plan team. Each team member wears a different hat. They celebrate success with us, they have been in our position before and will mentor us, they coach us, they will hold us accountable, and will challenge us to achieve more. It's important that we surround ourselves with positive people, and that these people provide insight, inspiration, and perspectives unique from our own. Selective diversity is pivotal.

For our career game plans, let's imagine the people we need on our sideline to coach us to success. Our game plans are long-term. Often, they extend three years. We will be selective and strategic with whom we invite to be on our career game plan team. Envision a huddle, where we have key players who will help us achieve our pivot line, goals, competencies, and actions. Who will be on our team? It's critical that each team member knows our authentic selves, inspires confidence, and will help us implement our career game plans. This team is the essence of strategic relationship building. It's rich with purposeful connections that will help us achieve our plan.

To build a successful team, I recommend filling five distinct roles. The best career game plan teams have at least one person who plays each role: celebrator, advisor, mentor, coach, and challenger. At times, an individual may serve multiple roles. It is more important to consider the objective for each role than the individual himself or herself. For connecting with purpose, I recommend: we (1) assess the network, (2) recruit the team, and last, yet not least, (3) build genuine rapport.

Stories

Amy, an operations leader explained her team selection process like this: "I select key people through sitting in on meetings outside of my department. I ask if I can attend, observe, and find people with thought processes similar and dissimilar to mine. I want a little of both perspectives. I am observant, and through watching others, I have found my go to people. I like to attach myself to the people that I want to mirror. I see how they have progressed through their career, and see myself as an apprentice to them. Others give me the confidence boost I need from time to time. They all help me to be better at what I do."

Diversity is an important ingredient in connecting with purpose.

A MBA graduate and brand manager, Kelly, took it a step further. She explained, "When I meet with my mentors and coaches in different parts of my organization, I always ask 'Who else should I be talking to?' I keep fishing until I get a name. I utilize my connections to bolster other connections. I summarize and play back my conversations to my manager and

Human Resources. I ask all of these mentors, coaches, and advisors for suggestions on my development plan and brainstorm short-term development assignments and shadowing opportunities to help me get to the next step."

Asking *Who else?* is a technique to build on an already strong base of connections, and find other purposeful connections.

Maggie, the executive director at Integrating Woman Leaders Foundation explained, "I have a plan of action before I connect with someone. Once they agree to connect, I have a goal before I engage in a conversation. I prepare for the conversation by creating a document outlining shared goals and priorities with that individual. It leads to better results, and connections that actually align with what I want. I noticed if I talk about my experience and then share more about what I want to accomplish, I build more meaningful connections. It is so valuable when done the right way. It builds deeper relationships. Follow-up is really important after conversations. I make a voice memo reminding myself about key details of the conversation right after, and then send a personal thank-you including specific details from the discussion. It helps me prepare for the next discussion, too."

Aligning our purpose with our connections is pivotal. Follow-up is essential to building rapport.

The leader of Mentoring Women's Network, Alison, shared, "I connect with those that have done what I wanted to do. I wanted to write a book, so I looked for those with that basis of experience. That is what mentoring is. I listen for similar stories with people, and then find meaningful ways to connect with them that are mutually beneficial."

I love this statement—*connect with those who have done what we want to do*—mentors are rich sources of information and guidance in career game plan implementations.

Nikki, the CEO of a networking organization, Rainmakers, took it a step further. "I connect with my mentors and coach on a regular basis. Those are the relationships that help us get to the next level. Everyone should have a coach. I leverage those relationships to share best practices and put myself outside of my comfort zone. Naturally, we do not want to feel uncomfortable, but it is really important to challenge ourselves to achieve more. Those that make us feel a little uncomfortable push us forward."

It is critical to find sources of reinforcement, but also those who challenge and coach. I strongly believe in surrounding ourselves with positive people. That does not mean that these people do not challenge us. They challenge in a positive, pro-active, and forward-thinking way.

Tools

We will use the following questions as a guide in connecting with purpose:

- Celebrator: Who will celebrate success with me?
- Advisor: Who will give me strategic advice (when asked)?
- Mentor: Who has achieved the success I will achieve?
- Coach: Who will coach me and hold me accountable?
- Challenger: Who will challenge me to succeed?

Assess the network

This sounds like something we might see on a technology provider's advertisement: "We tested our network and our network is stronger than theirs." This matters not just for technology providers, but also for our careers. Our network strength is pivotal to the successful implementation of our career game plans. It is important to note, if our network is not where it needs to be, we will get it there through our existing connections. Networks are like a web with influential people; they are the hubs that lead to other connections. Through intentionally connecting with those hubs, we will bolster the network overall.

Remember, we are looking for a team composed of: a celebrator, an advisor, a mentor, a coach, and a challenger. It is important that we fill each spot on our career game plan team with at least one person. It is certainly possible to have more than one person in each category, as long as doing so is strategic and purposeful in pursuing our plan. With the end in mind, let's openly brainstorm potential team members for each of these categories. As with any brainstorm, everyone is a good candidate initially. Let the names flow. Comb through social media sites and address books. Talk to friends, family, and coworkers to generate ideas.

Our career game plan team will help us celebrate, give us advice when we ask for it, mentor us, coach and hold us accountable to our goals, and challenge us to the actions we commit to doing. These are people we may already know, or others we have yet to connect purposefully with. I encourage us to be positive and limitless with the people who might play a significant role in our plan. Keep in mind that just as I have utilized stories from everyday women, our career game plan team is also likely to be composed of everyday women and men. CEOs and high-ranking leaders are nice to have in our corner, yet more important are the right players who will be available and capable of helping us achieve our plan.

Review the career game plan, and ask, "Who wouldn't want to join this team?" That will fuel the confidence to facilitate the right introductions and strategic networking to recruit the team. Before moving to the next step, list potential team members in the back of the book, circling those who are pivotal to the plan. Remember, individuals very well could fill multiple roles, and it is possible to have multiple individuals for each role. Think of the objective for the relationship, and then map the individual. It's more of a web than a linear process.

Recruit the team

The reason the career game plan is so critical is because it helps people say "Yes" to joining the team. Once they see the simple yet thoughtful plan, they cannot help but be swayed to join the team.

I remember when I started out in coaching. I met with a CEO of a large company and knew she would be an excellent challenger for me after one meeting. She asked really good questions that made me think more deeply. She got me to a deeper sense of purpose through self-discovery, with open-ended questions like "What else?" I asked her for a monthly touchpoint to help me with accountability, and she agreed. She gives me some of her precious, finite time because it is clear what I want to do, and it is aligned with how she can help. I have a clear understanding of my pivot line, my goals, my competencies, and actions that I am pursuing. She knows that her time is invested in a purposeful activity.

We know whom we want on our team, and now it's time to recruit. When done strategically, this is the easy part. If we already know the person, a simple email, meeting, or phone call is sufficient. Keep the communication simple and to the point. This does not underscore the importance of it. People have conflicting demands on their time, and while we might be tempted to share the full process, or our career game plans with many details, that can overwhelm some people. It is best to clearly outline the ask. This includes a little bit about our career game plan process and goals, expectations for the relationship, and some element of a WIFM. This acronym spells out *What's in it for me?* To connect with purpose, the relationship is mutually beneficial. While we are initiating the relationship, it is important to communicate the benefits for each person. We know we have selected the right team when we gain commitment quickly. If we do not hear back for a while, it might be a good idea to move on to the next candidate on our list. The fit is important, and if the team member does not see the value or WIFM, it's not a good fit.

For those on our lists with whom we have yet to connect, consider scenarios where the introduction will happen. There are a variety of ways to facilitate an introduction. The best way is through a common connection. Social media websites and networking events are great, yet often are more tactical or happenstance driven. I have met some great people through networking events, but I usually review the list of attendees and do my research to ensure I meet the right people. So, ask ourselves, *Whom do I know that knows my potential team member?* Ask around, poke around online, do some detective work.

Once we find our "in," I recommend writing a brief introduction for the person that they can paraphrase or copy into a communication quickly and painlessly. A good introduction includes these elements:

- Opening pleasantry reinforcing how we know each other;
- A clear ask to introduce us to the potential team member and why;
- A few short bullet points on who we are and one or two of our career game plan goals; and
- A brief WIFM for the introduction facilitator.

In the interviews, one woman shared an excellent process, one that I have implemented myself. The results are staggering. I almost always get a response. When this woman meets someone new, she stops to think about whom she could connect this new person with. If there is a purposeful match, she writes a quick introduction flavored something like this:

Subject: Connecting Good <fill in the blank> People

<Name 1>,

I recently met with <Name 2>. She shared that she is interested in <fill in the blank> and/ or working on <fill in the blank>. I thought the two of you could benefit from connecting based on your experience, passion, and expertise.

<Name 2>,

Thank you so much again for your time. I learned so much about <fill in the blank>. I hope you and <Name 1 > are able to connect as you have so much in common.

Happy connecting!

This has been a great template for me. What is also nice about this process is that it truly inspires reciprocity. I met a gentleman recently who said, *"I give to give."* Reflect on that for a minute. When we facilitate introductions for others, we are giving to give. While we might feel a natural benefit from facilitating a connection, it truly is intended to help others. When we help others, we all benefit. It reinforces our collaborative nature, and collectively helps all of us achieve our career game plans.

Build genuine rapport

With our diverse career game plan team recruited and on board, knowing our authentic selves will be critical to building genuine rapport. Confidence will be an important factor. Knowing our strengths, passions, and purpose helps color the conversations we have with our team. We express confidence when we share our career game plan and intentionally ask for support. By aligning our authentic selves with the team members' authentic selves, we achieve greater success. Women who do this well know their audience. An important skill mid-career is forming strategic relationships. Strategic relationships are likely with the people who will celebrate with us, advise us when asked, coach us, mentor us, and challenge us. Proper assessment of personality styles with our audience helps significantly. The goal is to have a good understanding of the team member's background and natural interests, and communicate our plans, and ask for input based on where that individual is best aligned to help.

With a "give to give" focus, this is not entirely self-serving. While we are the ones asking for the time, and gaining input and support on our career game plan, we are also naturally finding areas where the connection is mutually beneficial. A few examples women shared are highlighted in the stories in this chapter.

The overall trend is alignment—up front, ongoing, and in reflection. Finding common ground in expertise, experience, and interests up front and then aligning our communications with the team member produces a shared experience. Through a dialogue, we find areas we can partner and collaborate together. Perhaps we introduce him or her to others. The person might be looking for a new team member, a speaker for an event he or she is hosting, or for subject matter expertise in a certain area. Explore and align so that the connection is purposeful.

Women shared many best practices to building rapport with their teams. Some include scheduling regular touchpoints with the team member. The time sequence likely depends on the team member's schedule and quantity of input needed in the plan. There are many online tools to use to show open calendar times. I like ScheduleOnce. Tools help to eliminate calendar ping-pong and streamline the communication to focus on what really matters—building rapport.

Keep in mind the art of the follow-up. A strong follow-up communication outlines a sincere thank-you for the time, key takeaways from the discussion, and expectations for the next meeting. Specifically for coaches, many recommended phone touchpoints. By talking on the phone, we minimize travel time and logistical distractions. We focus our time more productively on the content of the discussion. It also enables better note taking. Note taking is highly recommended in meetings with our career game plan team. A voice memo following the discussion is a simple method to ensure the essence of the meeting is captured. Repetition works. The more times we hear and see something, the more likely we are to act on it. And, that's what our career game plans are all about—action! In order to take action, we must confidently ask for it.

Chapter 5

 Ask for It

Rationale

Our career game plan team is in place, and we have built genuine rapport. In the spirit of taking action on our plans, let's leverage our purposeful connections to ask for it. One important distinction here is that we are not merely asking for what we want—we are asking for it as if we will do it. The challenge of stating our intentions in terms of what we *want* is that it weakens our plan. *It is not about the want, it is about what we will achieve.* We will achieve our career game plan with the "will" attitude, over a "want" mentality. That's why our pivot line statement, goals, competencies, and actions are stated in terms of what we *will* do. They are not hopeful, "I want to do X;" they are affirmative "I am or will do X" statements.

The words and phrases we think and tell ourselves matter. The power of positive thinking is real. If we tell ourselves negative, non-affirming statements and cloud our visions with fears of not achieving success, it will make our pivot point journey much longer and more difficult. Conversely, when we replace the negative words with positive ones, the "wants" with "wills," and loop them continuously over time in our own minds, we will achieve success.

When women shared their dreams, they also shared their fears. We fear the unknown. We are human, after all. However, when we make the future more of a certainty and own it with our plans, we embrace positive change.

In our discussions, women overwhelmingly opened up about the fear they faced in asking for it. It is intimidating and scary to put ourselves out there. Some admitted feeling selfish asking for it. In light of the real fear associated with asking, many also said things like, "What's the worst that can happen?" This is one of my favorite questions in coaching. It is so easy to make excuses to not take action, or delay progress, yet when we ask ourselves this question, it all fades away. Many times the worst-case scenario is not at all negative. The pictures we paint in our minds matter. Confidence and positivity are pivotal tools in this chapter. Asking for it is all about framing the end in mind. We have our pivot line statement to drive us to an outcome. We have our career game plans with our goals clearly outlined. These tools promote the positive attitude and confidence we will exude when we ask for it.

We have huddled with our career game plan team, and are walking away from that huddle with our head held high. We're confident and positive about the second half. With our career game plan visualized, we're ready to play the game. Good players envision themselves winning the game or celebrating with their team, which compels them to victory. Good coaches empower their teams to play a good second half. They are calm, cool, and collected as they watch their teams play. As we should be, as we ask for the tools, connections, and resources necessary to play a good second half. Poise, attitude, and genuine confidence prevail. We will visualize ourselves achieving our success. It's pivotal.

We have a simple process for asking for it, first (1) prepare, then (2) actively listen, and (3) communicate intentionally. We'll be thinking about our career game plan teams and key stakeholders that we will communicate with to achieve our plans in this chapter. This process helps us prepare for the discussion and achieve successful outcomes through active listening and intentional communication.

Stories

A finance leader, Cindy, shared, "I have an elevator pitch. It's cheesy, but it really works. I simply state 'I want this and this is why I would be a good fit.' I test the story often to see what sticks and resonates, then I fearlessly ask others for help."

I appreciate the notion of being fearless. To ask for it, we have to remove the barriers and fears and replace them with positive feelings.

A marketing leader, Audra, shared, "You have to take the emotion out of it. I like to be very prepared for these types of discussions. Preparation makes me feel more confident. I use data to back up my points. I also make sure to not just talk about me, but the benefits for the company."

Let data be our friend. Arm ourselves with the information needed to support our plans and the purpose behind them.

Alison, a mentoring expert, commented, "Asking for it is all about understanding what would motivate your audience to say yes. It is important to clearly explain what's in it for them. When you ask for a raise or promotion, outline areas that are mutually beneficial. A simple open-ended question like 'What's your biggest challenge?' or 'How can I help you?' goes a long way."

Amber, an IT sales leader said, "In my new role, I had to negotiate my salary and benefits with the owner. I found it was important to have a clear objective, and to not be afraid of hearing "No." I reminded myself, the worst that can happen is that he says no. So much of it has to do with confidence and courage. Building rapport is needed before you can ask for it.

It is important to listen to the other's needs, wants, and pain points. Once you have really listened, then be ready to ask for what can help fill in gaps and add value to them based on what you have heard."

Listening is a very important attribute with asking. The ask is two-sided. A good leader listens before speaking. I highly recommend Stephen Covey because I love his mantra: *Seek to understand before seeking to be understood.* That's active listening.

An HR consultant, Catherine, confided, "A few years ago, when I was looking for a job, I did a job newsletter to update people on my job search. I included activities for the week, progress made on my goals, and asked for people to talk to. It not only held me accountable, but people wanted to help. I found a job quickly through someone in my network as a result."

This is a fantastic idea, and it certainly is a best practice for a job search if our plans go down this path. Having a simple communication plan and asking for help where we need it drives accountability and promotes the proactive ask-for-it mentality.

Peggy, a Senior Professional Recruiter, stated, "When I wanted to go from full-time work to part-time work, a coworker and I researched and wrote a proposal for a job share arrangement. We worked as a team, telling people what we wanted, prepared facts to support it, and communicated them very intentionally to the stakeholders. The company agreed to test the approach and the result was very successful."

Intentionality is pivotal. The facts we choose to share need to support our plans strategically, and align with our audience's interests.

Tools

Asking for it is all about proper preparation, active listening, and intentionality. In essence, communication. This is pivotal with our career game plan teams and our stakeholders. In this chapter, we will consider the following questions:

- What is the objective for each career game plan discussion?
- How will I align objectives with the individual with whom I am sharing my career game plan?
- What is my natural communication style?
- How will I actively listen?
- How will I intentionally communicate my ask?

With these questions in mind, we begin our transcendence from reflecting to sharing, with constant and tenacious focus on what we will achieve in our career game plans. Our career game plan team has likely given us some great feedback on our plans and helped us to connect with the resources, people, and tools that promote our plans. Now, it is critical to communicate intentionally in strategic discussions with those who will facilitate the plan.

Proactively prepare

Women spoke about preparation as a huge confidence driver. The difference is clear: when we feel prepared, we are more confident in asking for it. I noticed this during the interview process. I shared the interview guide with women in advance, and those who had jotted down their thoughts and answers ahead of time were often far more prepared and their answers were much richer. I also benefited from preparation. I looked at each woman's social media profiles, asked others what they knew about the person, read their books or blogs ahead of time, and decided in what areas they were most likely to help with the book's stories and tools.

When we prepare for pivotal discussions with our managers, stakeholders, or influencers, it is important to know our audience. This involves a variety of activities—talking to others to learn more about the person, doing some research online, or a quick chat with the person to gather some information to seed the discussion. Once we have done some up front legwork to learn more about the person, we can reflect on what we might have in common with one another. I think of the questions I might ask to learn more about the person. It is important that the questions are open-ended, and insight driven. We ask questions we could not easily find the answers to online or through asking others we both know.

I like to send a concise note a day or two prior to the discussion to align expectations. I leverage what I have learned from my research and clearly outline expectations for the discussion. The career game plan is an excellent tool that I often attach or copy into the body of the email, depending on the recipient. Some people are more formal and value this kind of detail; others are less formal and value the discussion more. The career game plan, formally or informally communicated, includes the information we need to share—our pivot line, goals, competencies, and actions. Our managers, stakeholders, and sponsors appreciate knowing more about who we are and what we will do.

A good pre-meeting note looks something like this:

Dear <Name>:

I am very much looking forward to our discussion at <time and place>. From talking with <Name> and reading <book, blog, website, social media profile>, I suspect we have a great deal in common.

For our discussion, I would like to learn more about X and Y, and share my career game plan with you. It is a one-page document I have been working on, which I have also attached. If you have time to read in advance, that is wonderful, yet not necessary. I will also bring a copy to share in our discussion.

I know your time is valuable and I appreciate you sharing it with me.

Best regards,

<Name>

One other tool women shared was the weekly newsletter. Although this idea was originally shared as a networking job search idea, the principle applies for our career game plans. Think about a regular communication touchpoint we could have with our career game plan team, managers, stakeholders, and sponsors. The timeframe likely depends on our career game plan goals—it could be weekly, monthly, or quarterly. The content of the communication is what matters most. What's wonderful about a communication plan is that it truly is proactive. We are not waiting for others to ask or take notice of what we are doing; we are proactively communicating our accomplishments, progress on goals, and the challenges we face to the people who are best able to help us. I encourage women to think about the following elements when building a proactive communication:

- Blind copy everyone on our career game plan team, along with stakeholders, sponsors, or co-workers or management in our current job roles;
- Write a catchy subject line;
- Share a brief introduction highlighting key areas of the career game plan pivot line statement, goals, competencies, and actions;
- Summarize key accomplishments, progress on goals, and challenges in bullet point form. People really like simple, scanable content. Keep it brief with no more than three to five bullet points. To test this, send it to

a friend and ask if she is able to read it in less than a minute on a mobile device. It should be that simple;

- Have a hook or call to action at the conclusion. Ask for it. If there is a particular challenge or action item that we are struggling with, here is the chance to ask for help. Be clear and concise with the ask. Bold it so if they read nothing else, they see the ask; and

- Finally, thank them for their time and support. Be gracious and show genuine appreciation.

Actively listen

Assuming we have prepared for our discussion, and informed our team along the way of our progress, we are in an excellent position to learn from our career game plan team and the influencers, stakeholders, and sponsors. Rather than begin a discussion with us talking, we begin the discussion with questions about the other person.

As far as questions go, I have a few that I love to ask, and certainly keep in my back pocket. Based on our research ahead of time, we should know a few key pieces of information that will help shape good questions, or helps us tailor our questions. Good questions are open-ended. The challenge with close-ended questions is that they usually receive short answers. If someone can answer yes or no, it is not a good question. Conversely, when asked with powerful question words like "how" or "what" we craft a strong question that yields insightful dialogue. People think about our question.

Some great question starters are:

- I see you transitioned from X to Y in your career. How did you make the transition successfully?
- I am interested in X, and know you have a strong background in this. For someone in my position, what would you recommend?

- I see you as an excellent <role> on my career game plan team. Based on your experience in X, I am interested in your feedback on my pivot line, goals, competencies or actions (be specific). What feedback do you have for me?
- Who else do you recommend I speak with about my interests?
- Based on our conversation today, I have learned X, Y, and Z. For our next discussion, I would like to talk about <topic>. What else would you recommend?

I believe in the "what else?" question. It makes people think. What happens when we ask, "Anything else?" Very few responses. "What else?" generates a much richer discussion.

Another important skill in active listening is being quiet. Yes, actually listen. Good open-ended questions elicit deep thought, and waiting the seven seconds for people to really think about what they want to say is pivotal. I count to myself; I look directly at the person, and patiently wait for them to answer. If I have asked a good question, they will need time to think about the response. Following a discussion, reflect back on the discussion and estimate the time we spent talking versus the other person. If the stakeholder spoke more than 50% of the time, we're listening well. I often am complimented on my speaking ability. What's interesting to me is that I speak less than 50% of the time I am with customers. I listen. People like to be heard. They enjoy when someone takes the time to really get to know them.

Communicate intentionally

This brings us to the next pivotal point in communication, intentionality. This will separate us from others. Intentionality means being specific, aligned, and nimble. The reason that intentionality is so important in communication is that, in order for us to achieve our career game plans, it will require many conversations with many people along the way. We can burn a lot of time talking to the wrong people about irrelevant topics, or topics not aligned with our plans. We need to maximize our time and be productive with it to achieve success.

Be specific with the objective of discussions. Just as we did in communicating expectations for the first meeting, for every ongoing discussion or event, we need to ask ourselves, "What is the objective?" It is important to reinforce the objective of the discussion to keep the guardrails of the discussion—this is about the career game plan goal X or specific actions on Y. Be specific so the parameters are clear, i.e., I will gain a particular input, new idea, purposeful connections, or advice. It needs to be clear what the benefit of the interaction will be.

Good objectives are also mutually beneficial, especially with our career game plan teams from Chapter 4. Communicating the mutual benefit to the other person conveys intentionality. This is not just a happenstance relationship; the reason we are together is clear.

To ensure we are connecting with purpose and with the right types of people, we need to be certain that we have found areas of alignment in the discussion. Based on our listening, and the answers to our questions, our goal is to have a few key areas of our career game plan that align with that person. This person will help us achieve our goals. For ongoing relationships, we have intentionally thought about the person and the role he or she will have on our career game plan team. Being clear in sharing our objective with the person is intentional. It indicates to the other person that we understand them and ourselves, and are serious about our plans. We are not asking for anyone and everyone's help; we have focused our efforts on this relationship because we see alignment. Clarity prevails.

Taking it one step further, one trait that truly separates good communication from the average is being nimble. Let it be a conversation. While it may meander, with good guiding questions, we return to the objective, and accomplish what we set out to achieve.

One trick to being nimble is the art of the playback. I love doing this. Usually, when I facilitate large group discussions with leaders, I ask open-ended questions, gather a few good insights, look around the room for more. Once I feel the room quiet, I do a quick playback highlighting the best comments that fit the objective already said, and I ask, "What else?" Paired with a playback, I always get a response from this question. It is powerful. People cannot help but say something. They have just heard a few nuggets, and are anxious to contribute; those are usually the most insightful comments made.

The playback facilitates a deeper level of thinking. It generates even more ideas. This is also where good note taking plays a role. Good notes capture the key parts of the discussion, so a playback toward the end of the discussion, pausing to look down at the notes, bodes for some really good dialogue. It often produces solid advice, coaching, or willingness to help directly. People like to be heard.

Before we conclude the discussion, we outline the next step and expectations going forward. This may be done in the form of a question, directly making the ask, or the discussion may have generated all the outcomes we needed. This is where thinking on our feet, and being nimble, really make a difference. It goes without saying that a thank you note or email is also critical to success. Recently, I have received several handwritten notes, and I keep them on my desk and reflect on them often. They leave an impact far beyond a conversation.

We are almost to the final career game plan strategy. Before we advance, complete the workbook questions in the back of the book. It might be a good time to reflect, edit, add, or remove items from the previous chapters. There is also an electronic version available online.

As we transcend fully, leading with influence is the accelerator. It provides fluidity to the process, and enables our authentic selves to continuously improve.

 Lead with Influence

Rationale

While the first five career game strategies have been focused internally on our reflections, and sharing our reflections, the final strategy is much more externally focused. It wraps all of the five preceding strategies together and catapults them further through leadership. Leadership is best demonstrated through everyday actions in real life.

When I asked women about the best leaders they have worked with, they often shared stories. They recalled times they asked for feedback, how they led a meeting, or how they communicated a decision to the team. There was not a list of specific behaviors; the women I interviewed spoke about actions in real-life settings. It was a part of who they were as leaders. It was genuine. Just like our authentic selves are built on being genuine, our leadership style will be, as well.

There are many benefits of leading with influence over leading through power. When I asked women about this, I heard that this was the preferred style of leadership, by far. Power is outdated. One advantage women have over men is that, for many years, we did not have a lot of power, so we have learned to lead with influence.

Today, many leaders continue to lead through power. Think of power as the *tell*, not *ask*, as a commanding, rather than engaging, style of leadership. People usually think of dictators, or managers they did not enjoy working for. And guess what happens when we do not like working for our manager? We do not stay. Studies suggest that 50% to 70% of our engagement is tied directly to our relationship with our manager and our leadership team. Engagement is a significant driver of the productivity, quality, and retention of a team. The business case is clear. Those leaders who engage their team produce better business results. Leading with influence is one way to engage the team.

The reason leading with influence is so powerful is that it signals to others that we are true leaders. Our actions are real. Actions speak louder than words. Who we are as leaders, and how we carry ourselves on and off the career playing field, is the ultimate game changer.

Review the six career game plan strategies holistically. See how the first half is about reflecting and the second half is more about sharing. The linkage from leading with influence to being authentic is clear. The reason it comes full circle is that in sharing our reflections, and leading with influence, we have likely come across some excellent synergies that further enhance who we are and our career game plan. It's funny how others always make us better. The power of collaboration has likely led to even better versions of our authentic selves. As long as it is aligned with who we are genuinely, we're in a better place. It's a continuous improvement process and once we complete the process, we come full circle and elements of each strategy come into play again. As others see our success, they want to come on board and begin their own pivot point journeys. We lead by example, which is what leading with influence is all about.

It goes without saying that the best sports coaches lead with influence. While they craft the game plans, they ask players for input and engage the team when they share it. Many high-performing individuals struggle to coach. Why? They know what worked for them and tell their players to do it their way. They do not maximize the talent of the team. They direct rather than engage. Good leaders empower the team and enable the team to collaborate. When a leader can influence the team to play collectively, that team achieves far greater success. Those are the teams that win the championships.

The recipe for leading with influence is much more fluid than the other career game plan strategies. Leading with influence is like the grease on our pivot point wheel. It is that fluid that facilitates continuous improvement. It is more about key principles than a process. There are many aspects of influence, and we will focus on the critical few that best align with making our career game plans successful. When done well, our success spurs others' successes. Our journey inspires other journeys, and we all benefit. For leading with influence, our focus will be on (1) vulnerability, (2) reciprocity, and (3) inspiration. At the crux of influence, these principles are pivotal.

Stories

Gwynne, a health care maven articulated the value of influence over power, "Very few times in a business setting do you have absolute power. Even when you do, be cautious about using it as a means to accomplishing your goals. Share your vision with your team, but also listen to their views on your vision. They are very likely to have great ideas to improve your vision. I remember a time when our company was doing personality inventories to help us all in our teambuilding function. We used Birkman at that time. I was meeting with my team and wanted to start the conversation off by putting everyone at ease. So, I said 'My Birkman states that when I am stressed, I tend to care less about people, and more about attaining the goal. Therefore, I can become rather abrupt with my comments and not very considerate when I am stressed.' One of my direct reports who had worked with me for many years asked, 'Do you think it took doing a Birkman for us to know that?' Obviously my team not only knew me well, but also was comfortable enough to say what they were thinking. I loved working with this particular group and was so proud of the results this high-performing team produced."

Self-awareness and willingness to be vulnerable with our teams truly engages them and produces results.

A brand manager at a global Fortune 100 company, Kelly, shared, "Leading with influence is common in brand management because people don't report to me, but I need them to do things to support the brand. I get to know them, and find out their motivators, and what they want. It is very different from design to supply chain. Over time, by helping others, and them knowing that you care about them, I gain respect. I approach people differently. For a more tenured manager, I ask what they did over weekend, or if he or she wants coffee in genuine way, and he gets my stuff done first. Simply asking the question, 'How can I help you?' goes a long way. Especially when done genuinely."

It is important to be genuine. Being authentic is deeply connected to leading with influence. This is an excellent question: "How can I help?" It is simple, open-ended, and generates lots of input when done in a sincere way. Leaders that lead with influence ask this question often of their teams. It exemplifies the "give to give" approach.

Nicole, a leadership-focused operations leader shared, "It's about explaining the rationale behind things. Sometimes we want others to follow without knowing the *why*. It helps them know why it's important. The 'why' can be how this impacts the team, the consequences, the benefits, the WIFM (what's in it for me). It's about explaining the story behind it to gain buy-in, and asking questions to see what the other person is going through. I like to remember the Golden Rule—do unto others as you would like done unto yourself. Empathy is so important. If you can put yourself in their shoes and show a sense of urgency, people are more likely to want to work for you and will work harder for you."

Questions are so impactful in inspiring others. The why is best discovered through self-discovery. Once team members internalize the rationale, they align with the team's purpose.

A political leader, Tonya, volunteered this insight: "As a leader, I sit quiet in meetings and wait for others to solve the problems. It's like I am sitting on my hands. If an employee starts to get on the right track, I may ask a question to help build off of what he or she said. I recognize that some team members need a course correction sometimes, and some may ask for the answer. To which I respond, 'I don't know the answer.' I really resent those leaders that just give the answer. It's so important to listen to others and help them answer the question themselves."

This is a true demonstration of vulnerability. It is very difficult for a leader to say, "I don't know." We believe we are expected to have all the answers, yet often the answers lie within our teams. This can be tapped into through inspiration with stories and coaching.

Tools

To best help others see our pivot point journey and begin their own, answer the final set of questions in the back of the book:

- What words describe my natural leadership style?
- How will I demonstrate vulnerability?
- How will I "give to give"?
- How will I inspire?
- How will I continuously lead with influence?

Our focus will be: (1) demonstrate vulnerability, (2) give to give, and (3) inspire. These areas are the most critical. A few of these principles we have already discussed in earlier chapters. Again, we have come full circle in our authenticity, and in sharing our plan and authentic selves, it makes sense to apply these tools now to our leadership style.

Demonstrate vulnerability

Vulnerability. In all of the leadership development training and coaching I do, trust is the biggest challenge leaders have. To overcome the trust challenge, vulnerability is the best tool. Experts like Patrick Lencioni have been saying this for years. To build a high-performing team, trust is foundational. Leaders are responsible for building that trust through vulnerability. One common misperception of vulnerability is lack of confidence. Let's distinguish these. Vulnerability is not about not believing in ourselves and what we will do; it's about being confident enough to admit our mistakes. We share our thoughts transparently, and admit our mistakes before others poke holes in our leadership. It is proactive.

Picture vulnerability. To me, it's like walking around with no clothes on. It's being transparent, forthcoming, honest, and bold when necessary. It's knowing what information is critical to share, and sharing it when the team needs to know. Sometimes, knowing what and when is not easy. At times, I have overshared with my team. It got me in trouble. My team really did not need to know everything I was telling them, and they needed to find out when the other teams did so the full team was aligned. I made mistakes. A good leader admits when he or she makes mistakes. He or she simply says, "I made a mistake. I did this and it did not work well. How could I have done that better?" Those that do this best are so in tune with their teams that they effortlessly model vulnerability. Once they realize they have made a mistake, they immediately admit the mistake, and, even better, ask for feedback. This makes leading with influence and vulnerability viral. The team members cannot help but mimic this behavior. The leader is vulnerable, so it is safe for the team to admit mistakes, and to be open and honest. As a result, trust builds naturally over time.

Give to give

In Chapter 4, we discussed "give to give" when facilitating introductions and connecting with purpose. I have thought about this phrase endlessly while writing this book. I am disciplined in my career game plan, and relentlessly seek to exceed my goals. What really drives me is a need for my work to help the women I care about. I genuinely want to "give to give." I want the career game plan to inspire a whole new generation of women leaders who transcend the glass ceiling. My purpose really helps me connect with "give to give."

Reciprocity. Rather than an exchange, leaders that lead with influence "give to give." They share resources, information, and their time to help others. Chances are that our career game plan team and other stakeholders we met with when asking for it are this type of leader. Observe what these leaders do and model it. So much of leadership style is learned through others' examples, both positive and negative.

To ensure we are giving to give in the way that others want, this principle builds on some previous tools. Asking good, open-ended questions to uncover what others truly appreciate and need, paired with being self-aware so that we are aligning our give with where we are naturally best suited to add value, ensures alignment. Imagine a mathematical equation where give to give = questions to uncover need + self-awareness to bring value. When done well, the result is a fruitful give to give where the recipient receives value. We feel good for delivering value, and the recipient feels good for having received value. In our journey of leading with influence, the "give to give" way of thinking creates great karma for us and our career game plans.

Inspire

As leaders, it's our job to inspire our team. We do that in a variety of ways. Coaching is one way to inspire our team. It's all about asking questions and inspiring self-discovery. When reviewing the questions in the workbook at the back of the book, think about this: What do all of these questions have in common?

They are open-ended. They inspire us to achieve more. These questions are intentionally designed as a part of my coaching framework. All coaches have questions they keep in their back pocket, and these are mine. They help seed the conversation so that my clients walk away with clear outcomes, and self-discover what they need to do in order to be successful. I could advise my clients, meaning give them the answers, but that would actually be more difficult. It would likely produce unintended results. Chances are the person I am coaching knows far more about what he or she needs to do than I ever will. I am vulnerable and ask questions to uncover what the client knows and help him or her discover it. The client learns self-reliant thinking that provides results far into the future. My goal is to coach clients to success, not tell clients what to do next.

Storytelling is a powerful tool in the inspiration toolbox. It has been a part of human interaction throughout history. It activates old memories and connects them to the new stories. As humans, our brains record information and file it away. Storytelling helps information stick. It paints a picture in our minds that we recall later. Stories also ignite passion. Good leaders do not merely tell us to do something, or just tell us what we did right or wrong, they illustrate it for us. Stories help us understand why we should care and why it is important.

I facilitate "Leading with Influence" workshops. We begin each workshop with an activity focused on the benefits of leading with influence versus the drawbacks of leading with power. The exercise requires people to reflect on the true attributes of a good leader. At a recent event, while storytelling was hot on my mind, a leader mentioned inspiration. As I often do in these workshops and in facilitation, I asked an open-ended question. "How do leaders inspire us?" "With their stories" was the answer. The leader then further drove home this point by modeling the behavior. He shared a story of how he coached an employee who was having a bad day, sharing vivid details of her facial expressions, her passions, the dialogue, and the outcome. I still remember his story.

Here's a story. I received feedback recently. The leader did not tell me directly *what* I could do better, but rather shared a story with me. He drew a picture in mind of the event, recalling details about my body language, my questions, and the customer's reaction. I could vividly see the situation unfold in front of me, and understood exactly the point the leader was making. In that situation, I was not listening—even though it's a skill I treasure! The leader was right. If he had merely told me what I did wrong, I might have backpedaled, made excuses, and gotten defensive. Instead, I saw it through his eyes, identified with his position, and self-discovered the point he was making without him even having to make it.

Let storytelling be one of the many ways we connect with our teams. The next time we communicate information, feedback, or ask our team to do something, brainstorm some stories to share. It will make it more impactful, memorable, and actionable when done well.

Good leaders do not tell, they ask. Coaching and storytelling are certainly great tools for positive discussions, where we illustrate points, and ask questions, rather than just tell our team what to do. There is an adage about leadership I really like. Good leaders leave a legacy. While poor leaders usually think that the team will crumble without them, good leaders often think the team will thrive long after they are gone. Those who lead with influence have given their team the tools and thinking necessary to make their own decisions, which has far more sustainable business results. The team continues its positive momentum even when the leader is not present. The team knows how to think independently, make decisions, and take reasonable risks. That's the mark of a great leader. One who has a legacy.

I will conclude with a question. How will we continuously lead with influence? It's the secret sauce in our career game plan. It's critical to being one's authentic self. As we pivot forward, we lead with influence through vulnerability, reciprocity, and inspiration. Embrace influence, and others will follow.

Conclusion

Pivot Point is about discovering our unique reflection, and sharing it with others. It's intended to be an authentic, purposeful, and collective exercise. The content of this book is designed to help mid-career women at the pivotal point in our careers. My intention is that women will describe their mid-career and beyond with positive, proactive words in the career game plans. Knowing that plans are critical to future success, and through simple tools, we will achieve more. I envision a community of women to share our career game plans with—gain perspective, join our teams, and help us succeed. I see us posting #pivotpoint on social media to describe our successes, ask for input, and connect with purpose. Collaboration is pivotal. We make each other better when we unite as a team.

As we have read, the six career game plan strategies are a continuous process, more like a circle than a linear path. Once we learn be authentic, express confidence, build a career game plan, connect with purpose, ask for it, and lead with influence, we close the loop and continuously improve our own authenticity, and spread the word to others. Leading by our strong example helps others begin the process. This does not happen in a vacuum; we all need to help each other to have collective success.

As we bring it all together, one final tool is storytelling. We just discussed the art of good storytelling and how it is an inspirational tool for leading with influence. Also, it is a self-development tool to reflect on our authentic, confident selves. Stories are excellent as we share our plans through connecting, asking, and leading.

When I began coaching, I discovered the power of this. I chose to focus on my authentic purpose. I really dialed mine in intentionally. My purpose is to drive increased team engagement and results through leadership development consulting and career game plan coaching. I believe in the impact that my purpose brings to the world.

Then, I shared my purpose with one of my coaches. In the spirit of continuous improvement and self-discovery, she said she needed more. As she dug deeper, I was able to find more areas of my purpose in my personal life, career, health, and financial goals. When piecing together all my goals and how it made me feel, we developed a more comprehensive story. It is a simple one-page story articulating elements of my career game plan, with feelings from my personal life as well. I reiterate the importance of spending time with my family and learning with my daughters. It's all stated in a proactive, future, internally driven tone. All of the statements are positive. I have begun reading it aloud to myself, and I cannot help but smile. It helps me feel connected to my purpose. For many women, our purpose is personal *and* professional. Our two selves intersect. My story does, too.

Storytelling is increasingly popular in corporate America. The rise of social media has made it easier to share our stories and hear others' stories. I challenge us to write our story by answering the question: What will I do? Let the ideas flow, thinking about personal life, career, health, and financial goals. Write them all down. All ideas are good. Then, weave them together in a short story that paints a picture of near-term success. Then, read it out loud occasionally. I recorded mine, and listen to it often to connect with it. And, I have been impressed with the effect on my attitude and ability to fulfill my purpose. I have made more progress in months than I did before in years.

Think of the conclusion of *Pivot Point* as the rebirth of careers. At mid-career, we have a lot of game time left to play. The second half is going to be a winning one. Remembering our glass ceiling analogy from the introduction, our intent is not to shatter or break it, but to utilize it as a tool for reflection and transcend it.

As we write our stories, we visualize ourselves achieving our winning career game plans, and through our success, we collectively change the game for all women.

Tools

I have mentioned many tools, resources, and people throughout this book. The purpose of this book is not to reinvent the wheel, but to leverage tools publically available to build our winning career game plans. For those tools referenced below, the websites are available to learn more.

DiSC: www.everythingdisc.com

Myers Briggs: www.myersbriggs.org

StrengthsFinder: www.strengths.gallup.com

Career Coach: www.findacertifiedcoach.com

Competencies: www.nielsongroup.com/articles/list_of_competencies.pdf

Patrick Lencioni: www.tablegroup.com

Stephen Covey: www.stephencovey.com

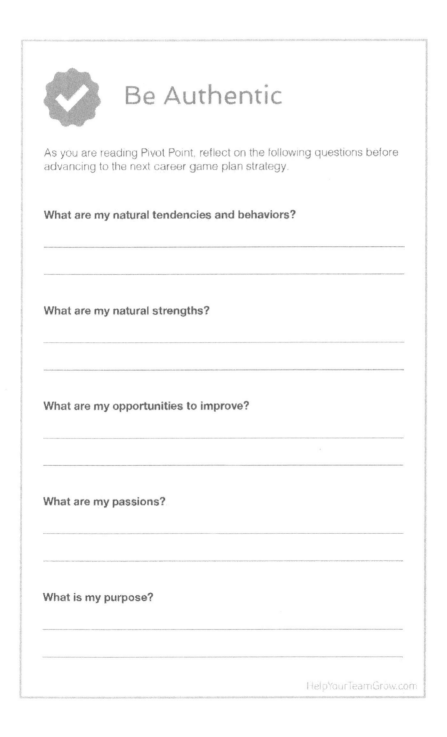

Be Authentic

As you are reading Pivot Point, reflect on the following questions before advancing to the next career game plan strategy.

What are my natural tendencies and behaviors?

_____

_____

What are my natural strengths?

_____

_____

What are my opportunities to improve?

_____

_____

What are my passions?

_____

_____

What is my purpose?

_____

_____

HelpYourTeamGrow.com

Notes:

Express Confidence

As you are reading Pivot Point, reflect on the following questions before advancing to the next career game plan strategy.

Who fuels my confidence?

_____

_____

What fuels my confidence?

_____

_____

How will I leverage these people or experiences to reinforce my confidence?

_____

_____

What people and/or experiences challenge my confidence?

_____

_____

How will I proactively seek out these people or experiences that challenge my confidence?

_____

_____

HelpYourTeamGrow.com

Notes:

Build a Career Game Plan

As you are reading Pivot Point, reflect on the following questions before advancing to the next career game plan strategy.

What do I want?

_____

_____

What are my goals?

_____

_____

What competencies are needed to achieve my goals?

_____

_____

What actions are needed to reach my goals?

_____

_____

What resources will I need to implement the actions?

_____

_____

HelpYourTeamGrow.com

Notes:

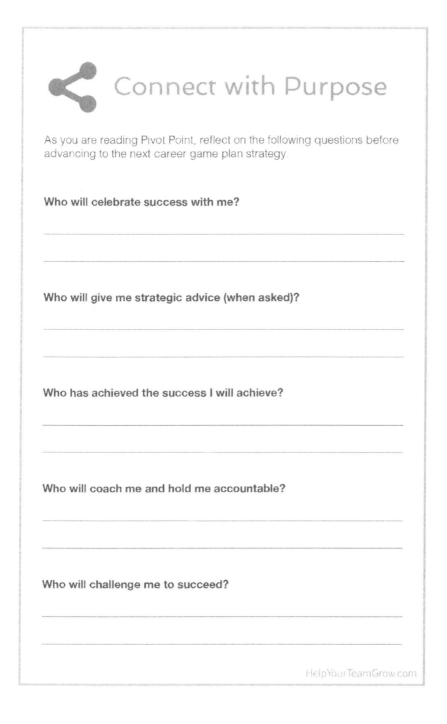

Connect with Purpose

As you are reading Pivot Point, reflect on the following questions before advancing to the next career game plan strategy.

Who will celebrate success with me?

_____

_____

Who will give me strategic advice (when asked)?

_____

_____

Who has achieved the success I will achieve?

_____

_____

Who will coach me and hold me accountable?

_____

_____

Who will challenge me to succeed?

_____

_____

HelpYourTeamGrow.com

Notes:

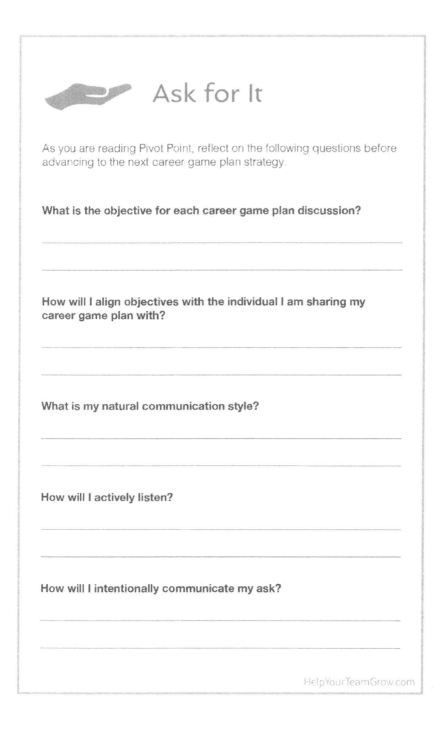

Ask for It

As you are reading Pivot Point, reflect on the following questions before advancing to the next career game plan strategy.

What is the objective for each career game plan discussion?

_____

_____

How will I align objectives with the individual I am sharing my career game plan with?

_____

_____

What is my natural communication style?

_____

_____

How will I actively listen?

_____

_____

How will I intentionally communicate my ask?

_____

_____

HelpYourTeamGrow.com

Notes:

Lead with Influence

As you are reading Pivot Point, reflect on the following questions before advancing to the next career game plan strategy.

What words describe my natural leadership style?

_____

_____

How will I demonstrate vulnerability?

_____

_____

How will I give to give?

_____

_____

How will I inspire?

_____

_____

How will I continuously lead with influence?

_____

_____

HelpYourTeamGrow.com

Notes:

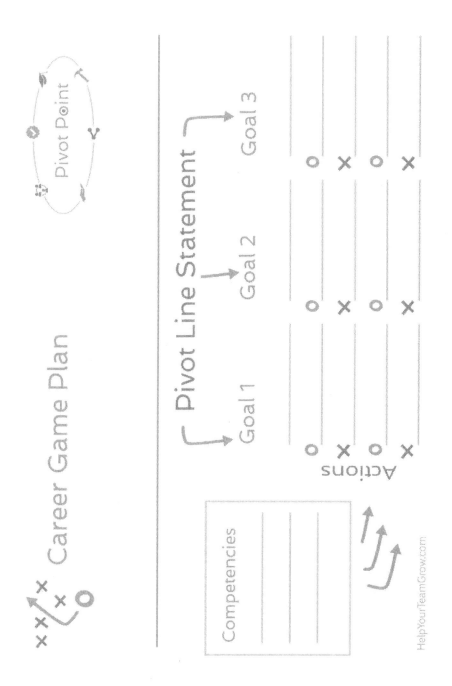

Career Game Plan

Pivot Point

Pivot Line Statement

Goal 1   Goal 2   Goal 3

Actions

Competencies

Notes:

About the Author

Julie Kratz has dedicated her career to helping teams grow. As a mid-career new mother, she made her own pivot point and pursued her purpose, starting her own coaching business. She is a Certified Professional Coach, MBA graduate, and International Coach Federation member with experience in operations, marketing, and strategy in the manufacturing, financial services, and agriculture industries. Through these experiences, Julie has been recognized for facilitation, strategic thinking, and leadership skills. By nature, she is collaborative, and driven by measurable impact.

HELP YOUR TEAM GROW

For more information on *Pivot Point* workshops and career game plan coaching, visit **helpyourteamgrow.com.** There are electronic tools to build the winning career game plan, connect with other women, and access the author's blog.

Career Game Plan Coaching

"*Pivot Point* has helped me tremendously. My biggest takeaway is the importance of having a plan. It all starts there. Once I self-discovered my strengths, and defined my purpose, it all fell into place. The career game plan strategies reinforced a more positive and proactive attitude, which has made a real impact on my personal and professional life. It really works."

- Lisa Wallace, Consulting Team Leader

"I have been working with Julie on my career game plan, and it has helped me express more confidence and prioritize what I will do. *Pivot Point* has empowered me to be a better leader, and focus on my purpose, which is to connect people. It has helped me to own my strengths and capitalize on them. I began a new networking community, Stiletto Network, to fulfill my purpose. It's been a real success. It's all about leading with influence and inspiring others."

- Amber Fields, Sales Leader